THE STATUE OF
Liberty

BY JON WILSON

Published by The Child's World®
1980 Lookout Drive • Mankato, MN 56003-1705
800-599-READ • www.childsworld.com

Acknowledgments
The Child's World®: Mary Berendes, Publishing Director
The Design Lab: Design
Jody Jensen Shaffer: Editing
Red Line Editorial: Photo Research

Photo credits
Brand X Pictures, cover, 21, 22; PhotoDisc_USLndmks, 5; Library
of Congress, 6, 9, 15; National Park Service, 9; Medio Images,
10; Centennial Photographic Co./Library of Congress, 13;
Carol M. Highsmith/Library of Congress, 17; Jet Lowe/Library
of Congress, 18

ISBN 9781623239589
LCCN 2013947400

Printed in the United States of America
Mankato, MN
November, 2013
PA02189

TABLE OF CONTENTS

★ ★ ★

The Land of Opportunity

★ ★ ★

In the late 1800s and early 1900s, many people in Europe were poor and out of work. America seemed like a land of opportunity where any dream could come true. People struggled to save enough money to sail to the United States. Ships were packed with **immigrants**—people moving to a new land in hope of a better life. The voyage across the Atlantic Ocean was sometimes rough and stormy, and life on the crowded ships was difficult. As the weary travelers approached their new home, they saw a figure looming on the horizon. A huge statue, the Statue of Liberty, reached toward the sky, greeting the new arrivals. The statue offered the promise of freedom and the chance for a fresh start.

This print shows immigrants passing the Statue
of Liberty on their way into America.

Frederic Auguste Bartholdi was chosen to sculpt the Statue of Liberty.

The Beginning

★ ★ ★

In 1865, a Frenchman named Eduard de Laboulaye had an idea. He proposed that his home country of France honor the United States with a special gift for America's upcoming **centennial**, in 1876. The gift Eduard had in mind was an enormous statue of a lady who would represent liberty.

In 1874, French **sculptor** Frederic Auguste Bartholdi was chosen to create the new Statue of Liberty. He sailed to America to find the best location for building the monument. When he arrived in New York Harbor, he spotted Bedloes Island near the harbor entrance. It was the perfect place! There a statue could greet newcomers to the land of opportunity. An old fort, Fort Wood, had stood on the island for over 60 years. Fort Wood's star-shaped foundation would be the perfect place for a statue to stand.

The Statue Takes Form

★ ★ ★

By 1875, Bartholdi was busy back in France working on small sculptures of the statue. He experimented with many small sculptures to find the best shape and size for the full-sized statue. He also needed a model for the beautiful, dignified face of Lady Liberty. Bartholdi did not have to look for long. He chose his mother to model for the face.

The French couldn't afford the entire cost for this large project. But the French and Americans struck a deal. The French people would pay for the statue, and the Americans would pay for the huge **pedestal** on which the statue would stand. Both countries raised money with raffles and lotteries. An American named Emma Lazarus wrote a poem called "The New Colossus," in which a mighty woman offers liberty to all who come to her shore. Money from the poem's sale helped pay for the cost of the pedestal.

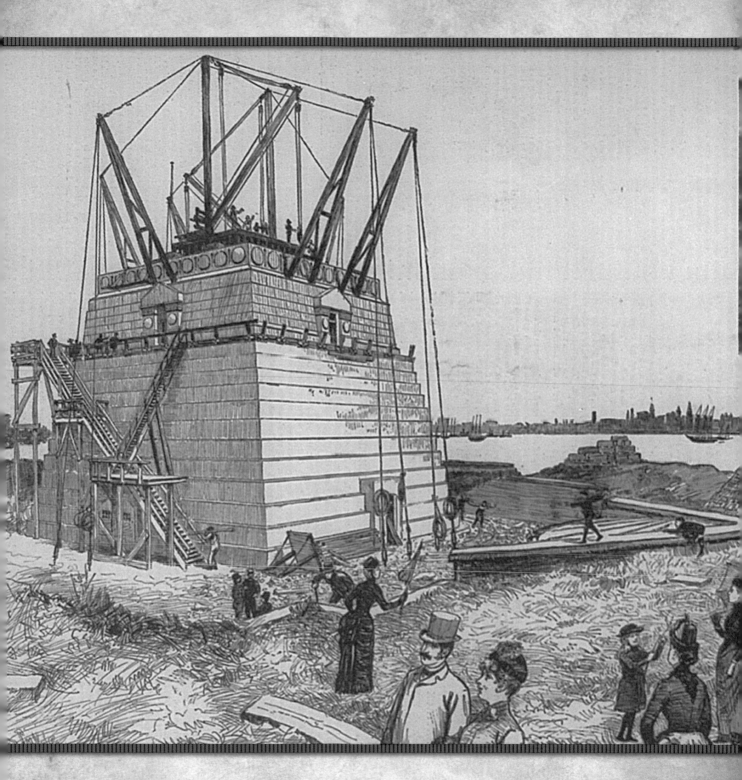

This drawing shows the pedestal being built on Bedloe's Island.

The hand and torch were displayed at the Philadelphia
Centennial Exposition in 1876.

Hand Across the Water

★ ★ ★

The statue slowly took shape. First a series of **molds** was made for the entire statue. Copper plates were made by carefully hammering the soft metal into each of the molds. The copper came from the coast of Norway. Each mold shaped a piece of copper into the right form for one particular part of the statue.

While the copper plates were being created, other workers were busy building the gigantic iron framework on which the plates would hang. This framework was designed by Alexandre Gustav Eiffel, who also created Paris's famed Eiffel Tower. By July of 1876, the large hand holding the torch had been completed and sent to the United States. It arrived in time to be part of the nation's centennial celebration.

Finished!

★ ★ ★

By 1884 the finishing touches were being put on the statue. When it was completed, the American Ambassador accepted the gift at a ceremony in Paris. The statue was then taken apart, piece by piece, and loaded into 214 crates. These crates were carefully loaded aboard the French ship *Isere*, which was given the privilege of carrying the gift to the United States.

This illustration shows how the statue had to be put together once it reached America.

*The Statue of Liberty could not be put together until
the large concrete pedestal was complete.*

Back in the U.S.A.

★ ★ ★

Meanwhile, back in America, architect Robert Morris Hunt had been designing and building the pedestal on which Lady Liberty would stand. This project would be the largest concrete structure ever built. For five years the construction crew labored to finish the pedestal.

Finally, in 1886, the work was completed. Frederic Bartholdi had the statue's many pieces removed from their crates and assembled on the pedestal. On October 28, 1886, President Grover Cleveland officially dedicated the Statue of Liberty. The statue gazed out across the Atlantic Ocean, ready to welcome immigrants to the United States.

A Giant

★ ★ ★

The Statue of Liberty is huge. From the base of the pedestal to the tip of the torch, the monument towers 305 feet (93 meters) high. Even without the base, the statue itself is over 150 feet (almost 46 meters) tall. The iron framework that supports the statue weighs 140 tons (127,006 kilograms). The 300 copper sheets that cover Lady Liberty weigh a total of 85 tons (77,111 kilograms). Within the statue's head is an **observation area** where people can look out across the harbor. To get to the observation area, visitors must climb nearly 350 steps!

The steps inside the Statue of Liberty are within a spiral staircase.

This picture shows the Statue of Liberty holding her torch and the Declaration of Independence.

Symbols of Liberty

★ ★ ★

The Statue of Liberty contains several important **symbols** things that represent values important to the United States. The broken chains that lay at Lady Liberty's feet represent freedom. The rays of her crown represent the bright light of liberty shining out overseas. The torch welcomes people from all lands to our nation's shores. In her left hand Lady Liberty holds the Declaration of Independence, the document with which the United States announced its freedom from British rule.

Time Passes, Liberty Stands

★ ★ ★

Over 110 years have passed since Lady Liberty came to New York. The statue still greets newcomers from distant countries. For the statue's 100th birthday, crews cleaned and repaired the monument from top to bottom. Today, over a million people a year climb the stairs to gaze out across the ocean from the observation area. As they pass through the pedestal, they see Emma Lazarus's famous poem:

"Give me your tired, your poor,
Your huddled masses yearning to breathe free,
The wretched refuse of your teeming shore,
Send these, the homeless temptest-tost to me,
I lift my lamp beside the golden door!"

These words remind us all that America is a land of opportunity, freedom, and liberty.

The Statue of Liberty was originally copper-colored,
but with time it has taken on a green color.

Glossary

centennial (sen-TEN-ee-ull) A centennial is a 100th birthday or anniversary. The United States celebrated its centennial in 1876, 100 years after the Declaration of Independence was signed.

immigrants (IM-uh-grunts) Immigrants are people who move to one country from another. The Statue of Liberty greets immigrants who come to America.

mold (MOLD) A mold is a container into which something is poured or hammered to give it a particular shape. To make the Statue of Liberty, pieces of copper were hammered into hundreds of enormous molds.

observation area (ob-ser-VAY-shun AYR-ee-uh) An observation area is a place where people can go to admire the view. There is an observation area in the head of the Statue of Liberty.

pedestal (PED-uh-stul) A pedestal is a base or foundation on which something stands. The Statue of Liberty rests on an enormous pedestal.

sculptor (SKULP-tur) A sculptor is an artist who carves statues. Frederic Auguste Bartholdi was a sculptor.

symbols (SIM-bulz) A symbol is something that stands for something else. The Statue of Liberty features several symbols that stand for freedom.

Find Out More

IN THE LIBRARY

Curlee, Lynn. *Liberty*. New York: Aladdin Paperbacks, 2003.

Malam, John, and David Antram (illustrator). *You Wouldn't Want to Be a Worker on the Statue of Liberty!: A Monument You'd Rather Not Build*. New York: Franklin Watts, 2009.

Rappaport, Doreen, and Matt Tavares (illustrator). *Lady Liberty: A Biography*. Cambridge, MA: Candlewick Press, 2011.

ON THE WEB

Visit our Web site for lots of links about the Statue of Liberty:
www.childsworld.com/links

Note to Parents, Teachers, and Librarians: We routinely check our Web links to make sure they're safe, active sites—so encourage your readers to check them out!

Index